With love,
Rafiq Gibson

HEY, GOD! WHAT IS CHRISTMAS?

Roxie Cawood Gibson
Illustrated by
James C. Gibson

PREMIUM PRESS AMERICA
Nashville, Tennessee

Hey, God! What is Christmas? by Roxie Cawood Gibson

Published by PREMIUM PRESS AMERICA

Copyright © 1973, 2006 by Roxie Cawood Gibson

All rights reserved. No part of this book may be reproduced or transmitted in any form or by any means, electronic or mechanical, including photocopying, recording or by any information storage and retrieval system without the written permission of the Publisher, except where permitted by law.

ISBN: 1-887654-95-X
ISBN 13: 978-1-887654-95-1

Library of Congress Catalog Card Number: 2005910358

PREMIUM PRESS AMERICA gift books are available at special discounts for premiums, sales promotions, fundraising, or educational use. For details contact the Publisher at P.O. Box 159015, Nashville, TN 37215, or phone toll free (800) 891-7323 or (615)256-8484, or fax (615)256-8624.

www.premiumpressamerica.com

First Premium Press America Edition 2007
1 2 3 4 5 6 7 8 9 10

DEDICATION PAGE:
This book is dedicated with utmost love to our Lord and Saviour, Jesus Christ.

Hey, God!
What is Christmas
anyway?

I've been thinking a lot about it, but every year I get a little bit more confused.

Is it Mom worrying about whether she's got all her shopping done?

Or is it Dad sweating out paying all the bills?

Or is it the cheerful ringing of the cash register?

Or, God, is it the good feeling I get in my heart when I hear carols being sung?

You know, God,
there are an
awful lot of parties
at Christmas—

Is this what
Christmas means?

Or is it the
commercials we see
on T.V.?

Or, God, is it my little brother trying to be good so he'll get lots of toys?

Maybe Christmas is Mom rocking my little sister and singing to her,

and smelling cookies in the oven,

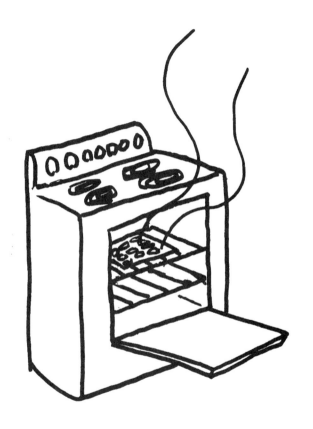

and the tree standing ready for me to trim.

But you know, God, some people think Christmas is sending out cards that say "Merry X-mas," whatever that means.

You know, God, we get out of school two weeks at Christmas—is that what Christmas is?

God, do you think maybe Christmas means hurrying? There's an awful lot of that going on!

Or, God, is it the story of the wise men bringing gifts to little baby Jesus lying in the manager?

Maybe Christmas is shooting fireworks and making lots of noise—

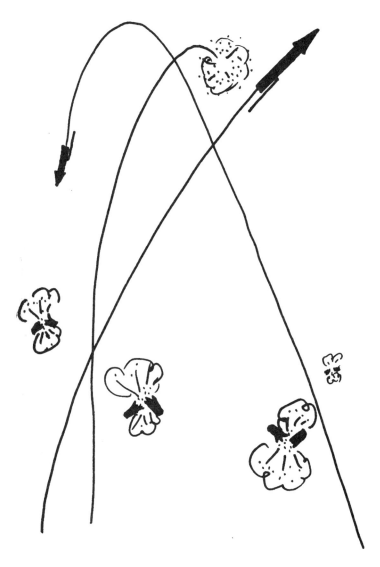

Or eating turkey and fruit cake?

But you know, God,
what I think
Christmas really is—

I think Christmas is
LOVE,

'cause when I hear the carols,

Joy To The World

and smell the
cookies

and the pine
branches,

and trim
the
tree,

and watch the
snowflakes fall,

then I get a happy feeling—

a feeling of love in my heart for everyone!

It's Your Love, God—

Your Love for all of us, 'cause You sent Your only Son, Jesus, to Earth so that I might be with Him forever.

Christmas is LOVE, God!

And, it makes me HAPPY!

Find all of Roxie Cawood Gibson's titles at
PREMIUM PRESS AMERICA:

HEY, GOD! LISTEN!	HEY, GOD! WHAT MAKES YOU HAPPY?
HEY, GOD! WHAT IS CHRISTMAS?	HEY, GOD! WHERE ARE YOU?
HEY, GOD! WHAT IS DEATH?	HEY, GOD! HURRY!
HEY, GOD! WHAT IS COMMUNION?	HEY, GOD! WHAT IS AMERICA?

TALKING WITH GOD (Board Book)   HERE HE IS (Board Book with CD)

ON GRANDMA'S MOUNTAIN

Other inspirational titles from
PREMIUM PRESS AMERICA:

ANGELS EVERYWHERE	MIRACLES
SNOW ANGELS	BELIEVING IN MIRACLES
ANGELS ALWAYS NEAR	POWER OF PRAYER

PREMIUM PRESS AMERICA routinely updates existing titles and frequently adds new topics to its growing line of premium gift books. Books are distributed through gift specialty shops, and bookstores nationwide. If, for any reason, books are not available in a store in your area, please contact the Publisher direct by calling 1-800-891-7323 or visit the web site at www.premiumpressamerica.com for a complete list of current and backlist titles. Thank you.

Great Reading. Premium Gifts.